Animals
OVER
and
UNDER

amicus
readers

Mankato, Minnesota

by Beth Bence Reinke

Ideas for Parents and Teachers

Amicus Readers let children practice reading informational texts at the earliest reading levels. Familiar words and concepts with close photo-text matches support early readers.

Before Reading

- Discuss the cover photo with the child. What does it tell him?
- Ask the child to predict what she will learn in the book.

Read the Book

- "Walk" through the book and look at the photos. Let the child ask questions.
- Read the book to the child, or have the child read independently.

After Reading

- Use the photo quiz at the end of the book to review the text.
- Prompt the child to make connections. Ask: *Can you think of other animals that are over or under?*

Amicus Readers are published by Amicus
P.O. Box 1329, Mankato, MN 56002
www.amicuspublishing.us

Copyright © 2014. International copyright reserved in all countries. No part of this book may be reproduced in any form without written permission from the publisher.

Library of Congress Cataloging-in-Publication Data

Reinke, Beth Bence.
  Animals over and under / Beth Bence Reinke.
    pages cm. -- (Animal Antonyms)
  ISBN 978-1-60753-503-4 (hardcover) -- ISBN 978-1-60753-534-8 (eBook)
  1. English language--Synonyms and antonyms--Juvenile literature. 2. English language--Comparison--Juvenile literature. 3. Animals--Juvenile literature. I. Title.
  PE1591.R466 2013
  428.1--dc23
                              2013010409

Photo Credits: Shutterstock Images, cover (top), 3 (top); Santia/Shutterstock Images, cover (bottom); Iliuta Goean/Shutterstock Images, 1 (top); KAMONRAT/Shutterstock Images, 1 (bottom), 16 (top middle); Pstar/Shutterstock Images, 3 (bottom), 16 (bottom right); Pal Teravagimov/Shutterstock Images, 4, 16 (top left); Sue Robinson/Shutterstock Images, 5; Michael Wick/Shutterstock Images, 6, 16 (bottom middle); Paul Aniszewski/Shutterstock Images, 7; Mark Bridger/Shutterstock Images, 8; Koo/Shutterstock Images, 9; Wang LiQiang/Shutterstock Images, 10; Serg Dibrova/Shutterstock Images, 11; Andrew Molinaro/Shutterstock Images, 12, 16 (top right); Thinkstock, 13, 16 (bottom left); Styve Reineck/Shutterstock Images, 14; BMJ/Shutterstock Images, 15

Produced for Amicus by The Peterson Publishing Company and Red Line Editorial.

Editor Jenna Gleisner
Designer Jake Nordby
Printed in the United States of America
Mankato, MN
July, 2013
PA 1938
10 9 8 7 6 5 4 3 2 1

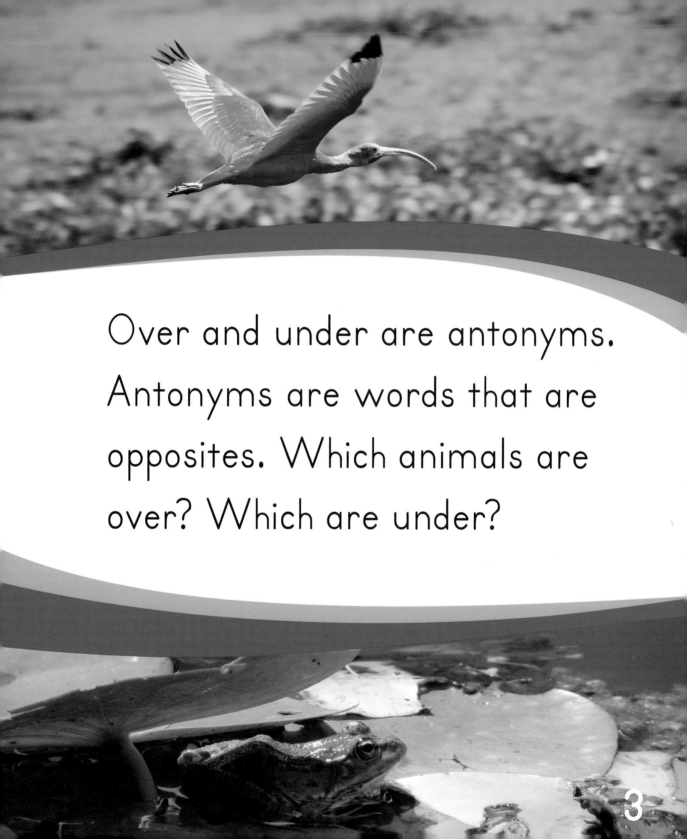

Over and under are antonyms. Antonyms are words that are opposites. Which animals are over? Which are under?

Giraffes can see over trees. They are the tallest animals on Earth!

Worms live under the ground. Birds pull them up with their beaks.

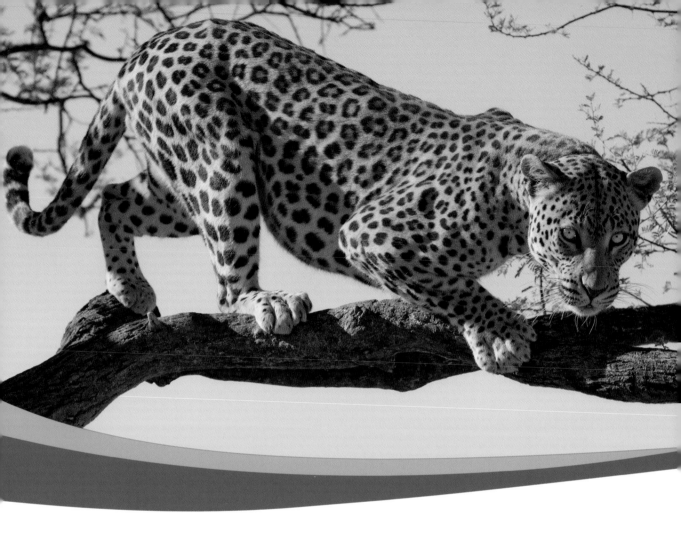

Leopards watch over other animals from above. They hunt and sleep in trees.

Frogs hide under leaves. Their green color helps them blend in.

Owls fly over a field.
They spot mice to eat.

Moles dig tunnels under the ground to find food.

Swans run over the water before they fly. They flap their wings and take off.

Stingrays swim under the water. Their large fins are connected to their heads.

Pelicans fly over water
to look for fish.

Eels hide under rocks.
They wait for prey to
swim by.

Bats wrap their wings over their faces while they sleep. They hang upside down.

Baby penguins cuddle under their father's fur to keep warm while they sleep.

15

Photo Quiz

Which animals are over?
Which animals are under?